www.raintreepublishers.co.uk
Visit our website to find out
more information about
Raintree books.

To order:
☎ Phone 0845 6044371
🖨 Fax +44 (0) 1865 312263
✉ Email myorders@raintreepublishers.co.uk

Customers from outside the UK please telephone +44 1865 312262

Raintree is an imprint of Capstone Global Library Limited,
a company incorporated in England and Wales having its
registered office at 7 Pilgrim Street, London, EC4V 6LB
– Registered company number: 6695582

Text © Capstone Global Library Limited 2013
First published in hardback in 2013
The moral rights of the proprietor have been asserted.

Edited by Daniel Nunn, Rebecca Rissman, and Sian Smith
Designed by Cynthia Della-Rovere
Picture research by Mica Brancic
Production by Victoria Fitzgerald
Originated by Capstone Global Library Ltd
Printed and bound in China by South China Printing
Company Ltd

ISBN 978 1 406 23909 6
16 15 14 13 12
10 9 8 7 6 5 4 3 2 1

British Library Cataloguing in Publication Data
Nunn, Daniel.
Numbers in Welsh. -- (World languages. Numbers)
491.6'682421-dc23
A full catalogue record for this book is available from the British Library.

Acknowledgements
We would like to thank Shutterstock for permission to reproduce
photographs: © Agorohov, © Aleksandrs Poliscuks, © Alex James Bramwell,
© Andreas Gradin, © Andrey Armyagov, © archidea, © Arogant, © atoss,
© Baloncici, © Benjamin Mercer, © blackpixel, © charles taylor, © Chris
Bradshaw, © cloki, © dcwcreations, © DenisNata, © Diana Taliun, © Eric
Isselée, © Erik Lam, © Fatseyeva, © Feng Yu, © g215, © Hywit Dimyadi, ©
Iv Nikolny, © J. Waldron, © jgl247, © joingate, © karam Miri, © Karkas, ©
kedrov, © LittleMiss, © Ljupco Smokovski, © Lori Sparkia, © Max Krasnov,
© Michelangelus, © Mike Flippo, © mimo, © Nordling, © Olga Popova,
© Pavel Sazonov, © pics fine, © Rosery, © Ruth Black, © Shmel, © Stacy
Barnett, © Steve Collender, © Suzanna, © Tania Zbrodko, © topseller, ©
Vasina Natalia, © Veniamin Kraskov, © Vinicius Tupinamba, © Volodymyr
Krasyuk, © Vorm in Beeld, © Winston Link, © xpixel.

Cover photographs reproduced with permission of Shutterstock: number 1
(© Leigh Prather), number 2 (© Glovatskiy), number 3 (© Phuriphat).
Back cover photographs of apples reproduced with permission of
Shutterstock (© Suzanna, © mimo, © pics fine, © Winston Link, © J.
Waldron, © Veniamin Kraskov, © atoss).

We would like to thank Gareth Jones, Eirian Griffiths, and their families for
their invaluable assistance in the preparation of this book.

Every effort has been made to contact copyright holders of material
reproduced in this book. Any omissions will be rectified in subsequent
printings if notice is given to the publisher.

Contents

Un 2

Dau / Dwy 4

Tri / Tair 6

Pedwar / Pedair 8

Pump 10

Chwech 12

Saith 14

Wyth 16

Naw 18

Deg .20

Dictionary 22

Index and notes 24

Un

ci

Mae un ci.

There is one dog.

siwmper

Mae un siwmper.

There is one jumper.

Dau / Dwy

cath

Mae dwy gath.

There are two cats.

esgid

Mae dwy esgid.

There are two shoes.

Tri / Tair

merch

Mae tair merch.

There are three girls.

cadair

Mae tair cadair.

There are three chairs.

Pedwar / Pedair

aderyn

Mae pedwar aderyn.

There are four birds.

clustog

Mae pedair clustog.

There are four cushions.

Pump

tegan

Mae pum tegan.

There are five toys.

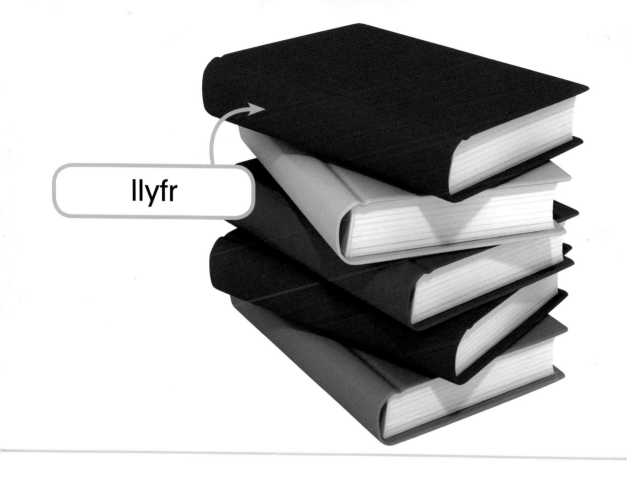

llyfr

Mae pum llyfr.

There are five books.

Chwech

côt

Mae chwe chôt.

There are six coats.

pensil

Mae chwe phensil.

There are six pencils.

Saith

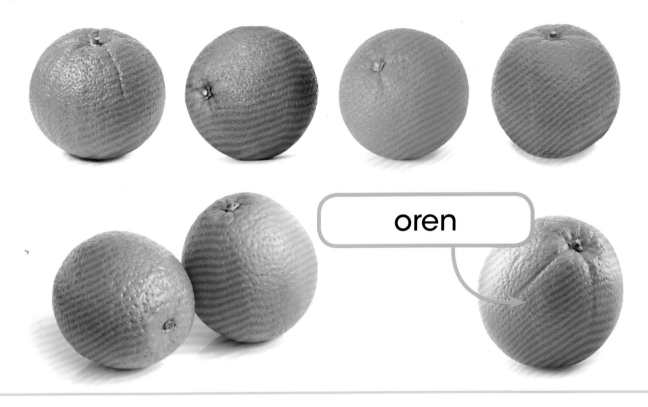

oren

Mae saith oren.

There are seven oranges.

bisged

Mae saith bisged.

There are seven biscuits.

Wyth

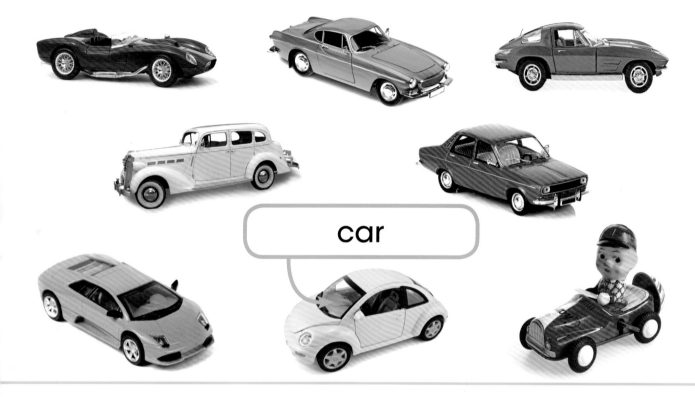

car

Mae wyth car.

There are eight cars.

het

Mae wyth het.

There are eight hats.

Naw

balŵn

Mae naw balŵn.

There are nine balloons.

cannwyll

Mae naw cannwyll.

There are nine candles.

Deg

afal

Mae deg afal.

There are ten apples.

blodyn

Mae deg blodyn.

There are ten flowers.

Dictionary

See words in the "How to say it" columns for a rough guide to pronunciations.

Welsh word	How to say it	English word
aderyn	a-der-in	bird
afal	a-val	apple
balŵn	ba-loon	balloon
bisged	bis-ged	biscuit
blodyn	blo-din	flower
cadair	cad-ire	chair
cannwyll	can-noo-lthl [1]	candle
car	car	car
cath / gath	carth / garth	cat
chwech / chwe	chwearch / chwear [2]	six
ci	kee	dog
clustog	klis-tog	cushion
côt / chôt	caught / chaught [2]	coat
dau / dwy	die / doo-i	two
deg	dairg	ten

[1] Note: "ll" in Welsh sounds roughly like "thl". Place your tongue as if to say "l" and hiss out of the sides of your mouth.

[2] Note: In these words "ch" sounds roughly like the "ch" in the Scottish word "loch".

22